A Little Book on Inheritance Tax

(or How to Die Happily Ever After)

Lee W. Denham

First edition published in Great Britain 2025

ISBN: 978-1-918424-57-7

A CIP catalogue record for this book is available from the British Library

This book is designed to provide information that the author believes to be accurate on the subject matter it covers at the time of writing, which is Inheritance Tax and other associated financial instruments specific to the United Kingdom, but is sold with the understanding that neither the author, nor any companies or charities that he is associated with, either directly or indirectly, nor the publisher, is offering individual FCA regulated financial advice tailored to any specific portfolio, or to any individual's particular needs, or rendering investment advice or other professional services such as legal, taxation or accounting advice. A competent professional's service should be sought if one needs expert assistance in areas that include investment, legal and/or accounting and/or taxation advice. For the avoidance of doubt, Investment, Pension, Insurance and Mortgage related advice are regarded as regulated financial activities, whereas Wills, Trusts, Taxation and general planning concepts are not, so different professionals may be required for each individual field.

No guarantee is made with respect to the accuracy or completeness of the information contained herein, and both the author, as well as any companies or charities the author is associated with, directly or indirectly, as well as the publisher, specifically disclaim any responsibility for any liability, loss, or risk (personal or otherwise), which is incurred as a consequence, directly or indirectly, of the use and/or application of any of the contents of the book.

This publication is intended for general information purposes only and does not constitute personal financial advice or a recommendation. In the text which follows there are some personal anecdotes describing how the author has achieved previous planning success in their career – these solutions will not be appropriate for everyone and the outcomes of such strategies will always depend on individual circumstances. Regarding the anecdotes, many people's names and identifying characteristics have been changed; any resemblance to actual persons, living or dead, is purely coincidental.

Inheritance Tax planning, financial advice and regulated financial products should only be undertaken following professional advice specific to your circumstances. You should seek regulated financial advice before making investment or insurance decisions. Tax treatment depends on individual circumstances and may change in the future.

The contents of this book do not constitute financial or other professional advice. You should consult your professional adviser if you require financial advice.

All profits from sales of this book will go to homeless charities. Please see website www.lwdfs.co.uk for announcements when this happen.

Also by Lee W. Denham

A Little Book on Pensions
(or How to Retire Happily Ever After) to be published 2026

To Anna and the boys,
who may not appreciate the old man tapping away on his laptop in the corner, but he appreciates them.

CONTENTS

Prologue

Chapter 1: A Brief History of Time and Inheritance Tax
(well, mainly Inheritance Tax)

Chapter 2: Catch 22
(Inheritance Tax – how it works)

Chapter 3: A Briton's home is their castle
(Residential property and Inheritance Tax)

Chapter 4: Love and Marriage
(Inter-spousal gifting)

Chapter 5: Good Will Hunting
(The importance of Wills & gifting to Charities)

Chapter 6: Trust and Let Die
(Gifts, Trusts & Family Investment Companies)

Chapter 7: Old Macdonald had a Farm
(Agricultural and Business Relief)

Chapter 8: Policy & Prejudice
(Life Assurance, equity release & investments)

Chapter 9: One Plan to Rule them All
(Putting everything together)

Chapter 10: Apocalypse Now
(Common mistakes with IHT Planning)

Chapter 11: The Future

Epilogue: final words

About the Author (what Lee Denham wants you to know about him)

Acknowledgements (of those without whom this book would not have been possible)

Notes

Glossary of Terms (what everything means)

Prologue

[Inheritance Tax is] "*a voluntary levy paid by those who distrust their heirs more than they dislike the Inland Revenue*" – Roy Jenkins, Chancellor of the Exchequer of the United Kingdom and Northern Ireland (1967-1970)

'*It is a truth universally acknowledged, that a single man in possession of a good fortune, should be taxed not just once when earning it, but again when giving it away upon death*'. It may be strange to open a book on Inheritance Tax by paraphrasing Jane Austen's *Pride and Prejudice*, but too often pride, thinking that talking about money is vulgar, and prejudice, in the form of misinformation, has prevented people from planning this tax properly.

In 2024 this was the tax that dominated the headlines, with the *Daily Telegraph* even campaigning for its abolition before looking on aghast as the newly installed Labour government's first budget saw the Chancellor of the Exchequer, Rachel Reeves, not only retain it, but also bring farmland into its remit, as well as returning the death values of personal pensions to the assessable estate of individuals, too. Fleet Street fulminated, while tractors and combine harvesters rolled up to the Houses of Parliament in protest.

Sadly, there is no silver bullet with regards to Inheritance Tax mitigation – and this book does not pretend to offer one, either. However, if you do not understand the difference between your Inheritance Tax nil-rate band from your Residential one, or are baffled by the difference between a living will and a lifetime trust, and how they can all play a part of proper Inheritance Tax planning, then the following chapters may shine some light into the darkness of the unknown. Similarly, the text aims to offer simple, practical guidance to anyone to ensure that they can plan for, and then hopefully leave, the type of legacy to their loved ones that they have always wished to do; it is not, however, designed to replace proper personalised Financial Advice, nor is it aimed at those practitioners of tax who should, one hopes, be familiar with all the concepts covered in this book already, which are presented in a basic, easy-to-understand way, rather than within scenarios that would delight a chartered-level tax examiner.

I have tried to illustrate many concepts by using those tales of the unexpected with clients that I have encountered during my career, some sad, some humorous, but all of which have been personally rewarding to me. At all times, the reader must remember that these solutions will not be appropriate for everyone, as well as that outcomes depend on individual circumstances and that taxation rules change all the time. However, it is my hope that after having read this miniature tome that you too may understand this tax a little better and will be able to put in place plans so to avoid [your heirs] paying it unnecessarily.

CHAPTER 1

A Brief History of Time & Inheritance Tax

"I am not afraid of Death, but I am in no hurry to die" – Stephen Hawking, English physicist and author of *'A Brief History of Time'*.

The idea of taxing someone for having the temerity to die is not exactly a new one and, like so many other taxes, was first introduced in 1694 by what is now known as the United Kingdom to raise money to fund yet another war against our traditional sparring partners across the Channel - the *War of the League of Augsburg*, to be precise. In principle, the idea enshrined within the *Stamps Act 1694* is pretty similar to what we know and (probably don't) love today, which is that every estate valued at over £20 (approximately £5,000 in today's values) at the point of death, had a one Crown (a quarter of a pound) levy placed upon it in order to be granted probate. That is, every estate save that belonging to the reigning monarch, which continues to be the only person exempt from Inheritance Tax to this day.

Thereafter, and as is often the wont of politicians, the 'tax' became a ramshackle collection of different parliamentary acts that, at one point, had land and *personalty* (any property that isn't land) taxed separately on death, with the introduction of a graduated rate to replace the fixed one to finance yet more military action, this time for the *American War of Independence*. Eventually at the end of the nineteenth century, a concerted effort was made to pull all the disparate strands together with the *Succession Duty Act of 1853* and *Finance Act 1894*, but it still meant there were three types of taxes on death, namely *Estate Duty*, *Succession Duty* and *Legacy Duty*.

With me so far? It will get interesting in a minute, I promise!

In 1949, the Chancellor of the Exchequer of the time, Stafford Cripps, made the observation in his Budget speech that, "*the Legacy and Succession Duties also have the drawback that they impose a proportionately heavier burden on the small than on the large estate*", so he promptly abolished them. If he was trying to make the system fairer to the less well-off, then he failed quite spectacularly, as can be judged by the budget speech given by another Labour Party Chancellor of the Exchequer barely a quarter of a century later, Denis Healey, who declared in 1974:

"Nothing is more offensive to the vast majority of ordinary taxpayers, most of whom are subject to PAYE, than the knowledge that people far better off than themselves are avoiding taxation by exploiting loopholes in the existing law. If the existing estate duty operated effectively, the great concentrations of private wealth would already have been broken up and with them many of the unfair advantages enjoyed by generation after generation of the heirs and relatives of wealthy men. In practice, however, the estate duty has always been a largely avoidable, indeed, a voluntary, tax. In particular, it does not bite on transfers of wealth made long enough before death to fall outside the charge.... I therefore propose to introduce this year in my second Finance Bill a tax on lifetime gifts—that is, any transactions containing an

element of bounty and including gifts in settlement—which will mesh in with the existing estate duty so as effectively to replace it with a comprehensive tax on all transmissions of personal wealth"

It Is interesting to read Mr Healey's words some fifty years later, not least since his criticisms could probably be repeated verbatim by many others in 2025. However, although his solution, Capital Transfer Tax with its rising tariff of rates, closed the loophole of gifting away wealth before death to avoid death duties, it was also deemed flawed since this also meant family businesses were similarly penalised. It was this main criticism that apparently prompted the Conservative Chancellor of the Exchequer, Nigel Lawson, to repeal the tax in 1986 and replace it with Inheritance Tax with a flat rate of 40%. If that looks familiar to you then that is precisely because it is the same tax that is largely in force today, except in 1986 the 'nil rate band' (the amount you could have in your estate before paying tax on it) was £71,000, before rising to the present amount of £325,000 in 2009, a level that will not change until April 2030 at the earliest.

Using the Bank of England Inflation Calculator, £325,000 would have been the equivalent of £500,000 in 2025 and this perceived unfairness was partially addressed by the Conservative Chancellor of the Exchequer, George Osborne, who in 2017 introduced what is known as the *Residential Nil Rate Band* (RNRB) that today enables homeowners to have (potentially) an additional £175,000 to add to the £325,000 already available as a nil-rate Inheritance Tax nil-rate band, albeit one that is subject to a number of stringent conditions which will be examined in detail in Chapter Three.

In more recent times, there has been a lot of noise in some parts of the British media about abolishing Inheritance Tax, calling it unfair and noting how the British version of the death tax is the fourth highest in the world, equivalent to the US that has more generous nil rate allowances, but lower than Japan, South Korea and France who also operate a *progressive* taxation system, whereby the amount of the tax increases as does the value of the estate, as compared to the UK's one flat rate. However, although in 2023 it brought into the exchequer only 0.7% of all taxation receipts, this still represents some £7.5 billion - which no Chancellor in their right mind is going to forego, at least, not in the short-term.

The conclusion to be drawn from all the above is that Inheritance Tax planning is a journey, not a one-stop, fix-all destination; governments change and politicians meddle, so the best planning in the world can be undone with one stroke of a pen in the Palace of Westminster. However, this does not mean that it is advisable to sit on your hands and do nothing, but rather it is better to plan, monitor and bend with the wind when changes occur. This book, therefore, aims to set you off upon that planning journey.

CHAPTER 2

Catch 22
(how Inheritance Tax works, who pays and when)

"*He was going to live forever, or die in the attempt*" – Joseph Heller, *Catch 22*

Everybody has to die at some point and when they do, the taxman is there waiting for his share of your legacy in the form of Inheritance Tax, or IHT as it is known in its abbreviated form. The taxman, in the official guise of His Majesty's Revenue & Customs (HMRC), likes IHT as well, since dead people can neither argue against paying taxes, nor evade them. More to the point, the beneficiaries of an estate cannot get their hands on the legacy until a solicitor has 'signed off' everything – this is what is known as a **Grant of Probate** and it is granted only once any Inheritance Tax due has been paid. Then, and only then, can the assets be distributed in accordance to the deceased individual's wishes which are usually, but not always, contained in a **Will**. This creates a rather comical Catch 22 situation of not being able to pay the tax the deceased person owes for having the audacity to die, since you aren't allowed access to their assets until said tax has first been paid. However, do note that HMRC are sympathetic to this situation and if there is a rather large IHT bill which needs to be paid that cannot be met out of the beneficiaries' private means, then they would be more than happy to come to a solution – after all, they stand to benefit too; more on that shortly.

At its most basic level, Inheritance Tax is very simple – it is a tax on your estate when you die and also be charged when you make gifts during your lifetime (see Chapter 6). Your estate can include your house and any other properties you own, savings, investments and any other assets. So when an individual passes away, the value of all their worldly goods is added up and any outstanding loans are then deducted to reach a total - and it is the proportion of this total that's over £325,000 (the current **Nil Rate Band**) that is subject to the 40% Inheritance Tax levy. It is only when politicians get involved that it starts to get complicated.

To be fair to them, the first issue of nationality is not of their making in a world where increasingly, foreign nationals live, work and then retire in a country different from the one of their birth. Therefore, with regards to taxation, the term used is **Domiciled**, which basically means if you have lived in the United Kingdom for fifteen out of the past twenty years, you are 'deemed domiciled' and so, on your death, all of your worldwide assets are grouped together for Inheritance Tax purposes. If you are deemed **Non-Domiciled** (or non-doms, to use their usual term) then, broadly speaking, all your UK assets are liable to Inheritance Tax whereas the remaining non-UK assets are not. We will be discussing property owned abroad in Chapter Three, but before that I would like to introduce you to George, my very good friend and client.

George, is a remarkable man. A boxing afficionado with an encyclopaedic knowledge of the heavyweight division, he can tell you the result of every single world title fight, not only who fought, their ages at the time, the weight and reaches of each fighter, but also in which round the fight ended. If you ever met him, you could be forgiven if you thought he reminded you of someone, especially when wearing a pinny – this time, another George, who first became Heavyweight Champion of the World in 1973 – one George Foreman. This George, however, did not need to sell grills or knock out other men to earn a decent income, for he had something that money could not buy and God could not divine; he had The Voice. Marinaded for decades in expensive rums and buffed to perfection by the finest Cuban cigars, George's voice was rich and beautiful and sounded like thunder rumbling over the horizon; whenever he laughed, which he frequently did, all the buildings within his vicinity rocked upon their foundations. So George put this beautiful instrument to work with his job and became one of the finest salespeople in the land, since nobody could resist his seductive tones; he really was the Casanova of Closure and legend has it that, yes, he had even sold deep freezers to Eskimos, who were too enchanted by his rich, sepulchral tones to resist his sales' patter.

However, there was also a dark side to George; he hated tax, especially Inheritance Tax. When I first explained it to him, as well as the importance of needing to plan so not to pay too much of it needlessly, he gave me one his 'George Foreman' looks - and I knew it wasn't because he wanted to grill some food for me. This was the calculation which so riled him:

Home: £1.0m
Private pensions held in trust: £500k
Final Salary Pension [Cash Equivalent] Value: £250k
Possessions: £200k
Savings & Investments: £50,000
Total estate value: £2.0 million
Less Pensions
(As outside Estate for IHT)
-£750k
Less NRB -£325k

Net Estate Subject to tax £925,000
Tax Payable (@40%) £370k
Net Estate after IHT £1,630,000

So if George were sadly to pass away, his death would need to be registered within five days, which would then enable the people administering his estate (his Executors – see Chapter 5) to obtain certified copies of his **Death Certificate**, that would enable his executors to liaise with banks, insurance companies, etc. to get values for everything George owned at the date of his death (including loans, too). At this point, a solicitor would usually be appointed who would complete the relevant IHT forms and send them to HMRC (form IHT205 for smaller, exempt estates, of form IHT400 for taxable or complex estates) and arrange for any Inheritance Tax to be paid. This must be done within six months of the date of death, or else interest will be liable and once HMRC is satisfied, a Grant of Probate is issued thereby enabling the executors to start distributing the assets from the estate.

Of course, if George was slightly cross with the thought of potentially having to pay £370,000 in Inheritance Tax, you can imagine how he felt when, in 2024, Rachel Reeves, the newly installed Labour Party Chancellor of the Exchequer, announced that as from April 2027, any unspent defined contribution pension funds left to non-spouse beneficiaries would also be included in the deceased's estate for IHT purposes, as you will note when we re-run the above calculation using the proposed new rules:

Home: £1.0m
Private pensions held in trust: £500k
Final Salary Pension [Cash Equivalent] Value: £250k
Possessions: £200k
Savings & Investments: £50,000

Total estate value: £2.0 million
Less Final Salary Pension
(As outside Estate for IHT)
-£250k
Less NRB -£325k
Net Estate Subject to tax £1,425,000
Tax Payable (@40%) £570k
Net Estate after IHT £1,430,000

An extra £200,000 now needs (potentially) to be paid to HMRC, with the potential added complexity that the scheme administrator for the pension has to pay the tax directly themselves. At the time of writing, over the summer of 2025, these added complexities have not been resolved. There has already been a number of policy U-turns from the incumbent Labour Government, so there may yet be another, and the conclusion from all of this is that it is important to work with a diligent financial adviser who has your back and is then able to guide you through the various changes as and when they surely come, because if you are a property owner, politicians have decided to add another layer of complexity to the calculations of your Inheritance Tax, as will be examined in the next chapter.

CHAPTER 3

A Briton's home is their castle (Residential property & Inheritance Tax)

"There's no place like home" – Anon

In 2015, perhaps in recognition of Britain's love-affair with property ownership, the government decided to add an additional IHT allowance of up to £175,000 that applies to the family home and it called the **Residence Nil Rate Band**, or RNRB for short. On the face of it, this would potentially allow property-owning individuals to have an Inheritance Tax nil rate band of £500,000 – except, as is always the case when it is left to politicians, the end result is more complex than it looks.

In the first instance, to qualify for this additional allowance, the property has to be left to a *direct descendent*, which means children, grandchildren, step children, adopted children and foster children; anybody else (such as cousins or parents), and the allowance is lost.

Next, for any estates valued at over a threshold of £2 million the allowance is progressively lost at £1 for every £2 over the threshold. This means for a single person with an estate valued at over £2.35 million then the residence nil rate band is withdrawn completely (£2.7 million for couples).

Finally, to claim the whole of the £175,000 allowance, an individual's main residence has to be valued at £175,000 or above – if its value is £100,000, for example, then only £100,000 can be claimed.

Having said that, recognition is given to an individual who did own a residential property before needing to live in a Care Home and, providing they meet all the other criteria, their beneficiaries can still claim the allowance.

Similarly, had they downsized to a cheaper property before they died (for example, if they owned a large house worth over £175,000 before selling and moving into a smaller and cheaper flat in a retirement village worth £100,000, for example), then the full allowance can still be claimed.

In spite of its limitations, the RNRB is still a valuable allowance. If we include it in George's first calculation in the previous chapter, this is the effect it has:

Home: £1.0m
Private pensions held in trust: £500k
Final Salary Pension [Cash Equivalent] Value: £250k
Possessions: £200k
Savings & Investments: £50,000
Total estate value: £2.0 million
Less Pensions
(As outside Estate for IHT)
-£750k
Less NRB -£325k
Less RNRB -£175k
Net Estate Subject to tax £750,000
Tax Payable (@40%) £300k
Net Estate after IHT £1,700,000

In short, the Residence Nil Rate Band is worth up to [£175,000 @ 40% =] £70,000 in Inheritance Tax savings; it is still a useful allowance, providing you have children –

but George did not, which angered him even more. However, he did have a wife; spouses and cats, as well as civil partners, are rather useful things to have when attempting to reduce a potential Inheritance Tax bill, as we are about to find out in the next chapter.

CHAPTER 4

Love and Marriage
(Inter-spousal gifting)

"Marriage lets you annoy one special person for the rest of your life — and legally split the bank account doing it" – Anon

The taxman likes married couples, as well as civil partnerships, and rightly or wrongly, they get certain 'taxable perks' once they have officially 'tied the knot', as my next client found out much to her very obvious annoyance.

I had actually *noticed* Elaine some time before meeting her. It had been arranged by her accountant that we should meet at a country hotel just outside of Luton and as I turned off the M1 at the appointed hour, saw blue flashing lights and a rather large traffic jam in the opposite lane which, as far as I could make out, was being caused by a huge, gold-coloured, top-of-the-range BMW parked in the outside fast lane of the motorway, its hazard lights flashing. Next to it was a very glamorous-looking lady, elegantly holding a cigarette holder from which she took the occasional, languid puff with the air that this was all such a huge bore and inconvenience to her. This lady, as I was to shortly find out, was Elaine.

As I arrived at the hotel a couple of minutes later, there was a message from her on my phone: '*Sorry, Darling – slight delay.*' Two hours later, the lady next to the gold BMW drifted in to the hotel lobby frantically followed by a load of worried-looking doormen who were clearly under the impression that this lady, impeccably dressed and coiffed to an indecent degree, was some kind of Hollywood film star that they had failed to recognise, so they felt the need to wait upon her hand and foot – just in case. Unerringly, she made a bee-line straight for me.

"Ah, you must be Lee?" she correctly asserted, before turning round to the now profusely sweating doormen. "I've found him, so you can all run along now, boys," she said, before turning back to me. "Terribly sorry for the slight delay Lee, my darling," she drawled. "My bloody Beemer broke down again and, you wouldn't believe, in the fast lane of the motorway – for the third time this month. I even recognised one of the policemen this time. It's so annoying when that happens, as it makes *me* late for everything – I'm supposed to be meeting my solicitor in five minutes, but instead I'm stuck here with you. Anyway, he charges me enough, so he can wait – and now I can ask him to sue my garage as well….."
As I was soon to find out, Elaine kept her solicitors very busy.

"So you are my next Financial Adviser, then!" It was the fastest anyone had decided to become a client of mine, before or since.

Now, Elaine may have been ditzy, glitzy and ritzy, as well as everything in between but, as I was shortly to discover, she was also one very smart cookie and a shrewd business person, too. Unlike most of my clients, she studied my reports to her, and unlike the few who also studied them, she also had sharp and penetrating questions about those reports. During one particularly tough grilling, I was taken to task over my poor soothsaying skills: "But Lee, my darling, everybody knew Mr Putin was going to invade Ukraine. Well, *I* knew – so surely you should have positioned my portfolio to take advantage of this? We could have made tens of thousands!"

She must have noticed me giving a deep sigh, as she then called out to the waitress. "Waitress! Waitress! Ah, there you are, my darling. This poor man clearly needs a cup of tea, could you get him one for me? And while you're at it, I'll have a Prosecco, please. Oh, by the way, you do look wonderful in your cute little black and white outfit – the waitress look really suits you! Lee, you don't mind adding these to your bill, do you, darling?"

As befitted her film star demeanour, Elaine's son was actually a budding, up-and-coming film director with an ever-increasing list of impressive credits to his name. Her long-term partner, Vyvyan, or Vyv as he was known, by contrast to his family, was much more laid-back and relaxed about everything.

"My parents hated him," explained Elaine one day. "You see, he was a punk rocker, with bright ginger hair and studs on his forehead. They said if I were to marry him, there would be no money for the wedding from them. So I didn't marry him – but we have been together for over forty years.... so we are as good as married, aren't we, Lee, darling?" As I was also to discover, Elaine had a long running dispute with her accountant about not being married to Vyv as there is (usually) no tax to pay when spouses or civil partners make gifts to one another.

It is exactly the same with IHT, with no tax to pay if you leave everything to your spouse or civil partner, as long as you are both UK residents; even better, this transfer doesn't use the deceased's nil rate band. So when the surviving spouse or civil partner subsequently dies, their estate can claim two lots of nil rate bands, which combined could then be as much as £1,000,000. However, if you're living together but not married, this allowance cannot be carried over on death.

"That is outrageous!" fulminated Elaine. "I mean, if I have refused to marry Vyv because of my parents for over forty years – that's FOR-TEE-YEARS, Lee – then I'm damned if I, going to do it for the wretched taxman. Surely you can do something about this, Lee, especially since you are supposed to be writing a book on the subject?"

Of course, I could do something – although I could not persuade HMRC or the government to change their rules.

The issue here is to do with how ownership of properties is set up in the United Kingdom and whether they are on a **Joint Tenants** or **Tenants in Common** basis. If these are terms you have not come across before and own a property with someone, the chances are very high that it is on a Joint Tenants basis, which means you own the property jointly with the other owners and that the right of survivorship applies — if one owner dies, their share automatically passes to the other(s). With Tenants in Common, on the other hand, each owner holds a distinct share in the property (e.g. 50/50 or 70/30) and there is no right of survivorship — each person's share passes under their Will or intestacy.

The problem for Elaine, in spite of her protestations of undying love and loyalty to Vyv, is that her home was set up as Joint Tenants which means in the event of her dying, the right of survivorship applies and so her share would automatically pass to Vyv and since Vyv was not a direct descendent, the Residence Nil Rate Band was lost. Moreover, since their home was worth over £1 million, the fifty percent share Elaine was passing to her long-time partner was also worth over £325,000 and so Inheritance Tax would be due on the surplus, since Vyv was not her spouse.

Surprisingly, the solution to this is quite simple. In the first instance, both parties must serve a written Notice of Severance to the other(s), that must be properly signed and dated, optimally using Form SEV from HM Land Registry. This is then submitted to HM Land Registry along with Form AP1 which adds a restriction to the title (Form A restriction), that confirms the owners now hold as Tenants in Common. Once Elaine has done this, she can then change her will by adding the instruction that upon her death, her share of the residential home is passed directly to Chris and since he is her son and therefore a direct descendant, Elaine can now claim and use her RNRB allowance, while Vyv is allowed to remain in the residence as a life tenant of a Protective Property Trust (see Chapter 6). It is not an ideal solution and there may still be IHT to pay – however, what this all demonstrates is that with proper planning, all the available allowances can be utilised while property and other assets can be passed to the right beneficiaries in the correct way - and the best way to ensure all of this happens, is with a Will.

CHAPTER 5

Good Will Hunting
(The importance of Wills & gifting to Charities)

"Where there's a will, there's a way" – Anon

Wills are very important. Actually, everybody knows this, which makes it all the more perplexing that hardly anyone has one. Indeed, according to research from Canada Life, half of all adults don't have a will (source: https://www.canadalife.co.uk/pensionhub-news/half-of-uk-adults-don-t-have-a-will/) and, unsurprisingly, the majority of those who do are over the age of 55.

Indeed, at this point my clients Dottie and Ted come to mind - not least, the looks on their faces whenever I paid them a visit to talk about their pensions and plans for retirement. As we sat down around the kitchen table, they would look at me rather sheepishly.

"Lee, we are very sorry ….." Dottie would begin.
"We did intend to do it," continued Ted. "In fact, the other night, we even sat down together and said, this time, we must definitely do it."
"We tried …" said Dottie.
"And we actually removed it from the cellophane wrapper, so that's a start," added Ted, triumphantly.

They were, of course, referring to their Will[See Notes 1], bought from WH Smiths. Since it was a relatively simple estate – upon the first death, everything would be passed to the survivor, whereas on their death all that was left was to be split equally between their nieces and nephews – it was decided that they would do it themselves. Except, even with the best of intentions, they didn't – which would perhaps go some way to explaining why I then studied to become a Will Writer in addition to my other qualifications.

Planning to avoid paying unnecessary Inheritance Tax is important, but there's no point if after you die your assets are distributed differently from how you would have wished, even if it is in the most tax-efficient way. A Will does this, as it tells those dealing with your estate where you want your wealth to go after you pass away and so by putting your wishes in writing, everyone is clear who you want to benefit from your estate, saving your loved ones time, money and stress. Without a Will, your estate will be distributed according to the Laws of Intestacy, which may not be as you intended or very tax efficient, as Elaine found out in the previous chapter, or your wealth may be funnelled to relatives in ways you didn't expect, and not necessarily to those who you wanted to benefit. You can find out more about the laws of intestacy in the following link: https://www.gov.uk/inherits-someonedies-without-will . These rules differ based on where you live UK.

An example of poor, non-existent planning can be illustrated in this short, quite tragic, yet cautionary tale. It concerns a small close-knit family of three, a mother, Rosie, her husband Jim, and their son, Chuck, who suffered terribly when he came home from school one day as a young teenager to discover his father had been killed at work that afternoon. The financial compensation of death in service and the life assurance policies did not matter a jot when compared to the priceless loss of his father, in spite of the fact he and his mother were now financially reasonably well-off; tragically, he suffered a small breakdown and struggled at school thereafter. Time heals though and eventually his mother, Rosie, found another man, named John, who brilliantly and cheerfully took on the role of step-father to the young lad who, in turn idolised him especially when he was asked to be the best-man when John and Rosie eventually got married. However, tragedy was to strike again when Rosie was diagnosed with cancer and she too passed away. Virtually the entire family wealth was tied up in the main residence, which was on a Joint Tenancy basis between the young lad's late mother and his step-father, John, who now 'inherited' everything. Money does strange things to people and when John got together with a new girlfriend and she didn't want anything to do with Chuck, John gave him £10,000 and told him to leave the former home of his late parents. John now no longer wants anything to do with his step-son and is now living in the same house with his new girlfriend.

This family were not clients of mine, but lived in the same town. Even so, it does not need to spelt out here what should have happened morally and what could have been achieved if careful financial planning had been engaged from the outset. This is not a unique phenomenon, so much so that it has its own term, which is *sideways disinheritance*. Either way, it does prove that money brings out the worst in people, so if this story does not hammer home the importance of planning and wills – and not just talking about them – then I really don't know what would; you need to be making sure your Financial Adviser is ensuring this happens at your next planning meeting, at the latest.

Writing and executing a will then is an act of pure self-sacrifice, entirely for the benefit of others. It won't make any difference to how or when you're going to die but it does provide huge advantages for those you leave behind, not least protecting your loved ones and making it easier for them at a difficult time. Your Will can appoint guardians for minor children, make provision for non-family members and unmarried partners, appoint individuals to manage your estate, avoid family feuds and hopefully avoid further tragic stories, such as the fate that befell Chuck.

At a basic level, it is not a complex document. The person writing the will, the **testator**, indicates what they would like to happen to their assets upon their death and who they would like to have them (the **beneficiaries**). They appoint people to carry out these instruction, usually close family or friends ideally younger than they are for obvious reasons and these are called the **executors**. Providing the document is then signed and witnessed by two people (or just the one in Scotland), it is a valid will. Contrary to common belief, it does not need to be dated, although ideally it should be, especially if more than one has been written during the lifetime of the testator.

That said, anything more than a simple Will probably needs an expert hand along the way, which can be demonstrated by a cautionary tale using Wills for charitable giving. Many reading this would probably have seen advertisements, particularly on television, that encourage leaving a lump sum on death to a charity – indeed, this is an initiative supported by the government to the extent that if an individual leaves 10% or more of their estate to a [registered] charity (or political party) via their Will, their IHT bill can be reduced by 10% as well - in other words the estate is taxed at 36%, not 40%.

However, in typical UK tax fashion, this has become more needlessly complex than it ever intended to be. This is because the 10% charity legislation precedes the laws outlining the Residential Nil Rate band which, combined with meddling ministers and short-sighted civil servants not employing joined-up thinking, have caused unforeseen outcomes for the unwary. As a consequence, in order for a Will to currently qualify for the 10% discount, the charitable gift has to be at least 10% of the *baseline amount*, which is the amount of the total estate less the IHT nil rate band of £325,000, but ignoring the £175,000 of the Residential Nil Rate band. This is the critical point; I have seen old Wills with the phrase "*I bequeath 10% of my taxable estate to charity*" which means the estate less both the IHT Nil Rate band and the Residential Nil Rate band and so will therefore fail to receive any relief, as well as a mere "*10% of my estate*" which can be interpreted as the entire amount before any of the reliefs have been applied. In order to avoid this mess. most Wills now use wording like "*such sum as secures the reduced rate*" to avoid this trap but, of course, if you didn't know this in the first place it just will not be there.

Happily, any decent probate solicitor is well able to iron out such calamitous outcomes by use of a **Deed of Variation**, which is a mechanism that can alter a Will after the testator has died. There are, however, some stipulations, including that one can be enacted only within two years of the deceased person's passing and that any changes must be agreed upon by all beneficiaries who are all of sound mind and over the age of eighteen. Therefore, it is not fool-proof and also comes with extra legal costs and headaches.

Once a will is complete that is not necessarily the end of the story. There is no point in having a perfectly written will that would execute your wishes perfectly, if nobody can find it on your death, so you need to ensure that it is recorded with The National Will Register (www.nationalwillregister.co.uk), that your loved ones know it exists and that it is regularly reviewed, not least since something as 'innocent' as getting married can invalidate an existing will.

Indeed, in May 2025, the Law Commission published its Modernising Wills Law Report, featuring thirty one recommendations and a draft Bill intended to overhaul the current legislation covered by the Wills Act that was enacted, incredibly, in 1837, where it is proposed that wills should become electronic with remote witnessing, along with changes to the minimum age a will can be written (currently at the age of eighteen). Things change – remember the words from the opening of this book, where I said Inheritance Tax planning is a journey, not a one-stop destination; so don't be caught out.

CHAPTER 6

Trust and Let Die
(Gifts, Trusts & Family Investment Companies)

"We make a living by what we get, but we make a life by what we give" — Winston Churchill, Prime Minister of the United Kingdom & Northern Ireland (1940-45, 1951-55)

Talk to any decent Financial Adviser about one of the hardest things they have to do in their jobs and, invariably, the subject of *gifting* will be mentioned. Very often with Inheritance Tax planning, the individual(s) concerned are usually of an age who remember some difficult times in recent British history; the rationing after the war years, the 1970s when Britain was regarded as the 'sick man of Europe' with its declining economy being held to ransom by striking workers, as well as one day in October 1989 – commonly referred to as Black Wednesday – when interest rates shot up from 10% in the morning, to 15% by the end of the working day. So these people are not going to start gifting away their hard-earned assets and money easily, reasoning that their heirs will at least get "*sixty percent of something.*" To be frank, you cannot doubt the soundness of the conclusion and so often my warning that "*you don't want to be the richest person in the graveyard*" falls upon deaf ears.

At this point in the book, it may be wise to pause and acknowledge that there are many greater problems in life than making decisions as to whether or not to gift wealth away to avoid paying tax on death. During a time the British media labels a 'cost of living crisis' with food banks, as well as unaffordable mortgages and rents common topics of discussion, I am not blind to the fact that I am writing a book educating people on how to avoid paying a tax that may go some way towards remedying that situation - so all profits from this book will be donated to homeless charities, since one of their many missions focuses on homeless people whose situation probably means most of them won't ever need to pay Inheritance Tax, whether they wanted to or not.

Working closely with a Financial Adviser, in particular one who uses Cashflow Modelling as part of their standard working practice (and really if your Financial Adviser is not, then what are you paying them for ?), should establish very quickly if it is possible and prudent for an individual to even start considering giving assets away as part of an Inheritance Tax mitigation strategy, as well as how much they can afford to do so. We will be considering this more in Chapter 10 that deals with putting it all together into a plan, but in the short term, there are certain amounts you can gift over an annual period that would be disregarded for IHT purposes and these include:

• Every person has an annual gifting allowance of £3,000 each tax year, which can be to just one individual or a number of people;

• This allowance can be carried forward from the previous year if it has not been used, meaning there is the potential to give up to £6,000 in one gift. Although this means you can only carry forward any unused allowance for one year, it also means that married couples and civil partners could give away up to £12,000 at once using these allowances;

• It is also possible for an individual to make as many small gifts of up to £250 as they wish, although not to the same person, or to the person who benefitted from the annual gifting allowance;

• Gifts between spouses and civil partners of any size are also exempt.

In addition to this, in the event of a wedding, the following further gifts can be made:

• £5,000 to your child who is getting married;
• £2,500 to your grandchild or great-grandchild;
• £2,500 to your spouse or civil partner-to-be;
• £1,000 to any other person.

Now the above are all gifts from an individual's capital, which in layman's terms would be the equivalent of 'savings', as opposed to 'income' where it is theoretically possible to gift unlimited amounts of money to another person with no immediate or potential liability to IHT. The amount of the gift is not capped, providing you can meet the following rules:

• that the gift has been made from income, not capital;
• does not impact upon your usual standard of living;
• is of a regular pattern, for example, monthly or annually.

Theoretically this means an individual could pay for one, or all, of their grandchildren's extra-curricular school lessons or fees, or even give them an allowance while at university. However, they must always be mindful of the rules – and scrutiny of their bank statements will always reveal the truth, especially since HMRC adopts an approach of 'guilty until proven otherwise'.

Any gifts that fall outside the above lists, then become what is known as a **Potentially Exempt Transfer**, or PET to use its commonly used acronym. It is 'potentially exempt' since, providing the person making the gift lives a further seven years of more, it then falls outside of their estate for IHT. However, if they were to die within those seven years, then it becomes what is known as a 'Failed PET' and is returned back into the estate to be assessed for any IHT liability. Recognition is given, on a sliding scale (known as **taper relief**), that there is difference if an individual gifted something and lived for six years and three hundred and sixty days, as opposed to one who only lived a mere six days after making the gift, that reduces the tax due, although, do note that the liability is then the responsibility of the individual who received the gift, not the executors of the deceased's estate. In the case of the biggest gifts, insurance can be taken out to cover any potential tax bill and this insurance is called *gift inter vivos* insurance.

One of the most commonly cited reasons people use to explain their reluctance to gift money away, even if they do tacitly agree that they no longer need so much, is lack of *control* – the fear that by gifting it to their married children that they are either cannot be trusted with the money, or they have spouses/civil-partners where in the event of a divorce, part of the 'family wealth' may disappear when the divorce judge, inevitably, splits all assets 50/50. In these situations, the answer is a Financial Adviser's best friend and an amateur DIY investor's worst enemy; a **Trust**.

A Trust[See Notes 2] has been described, somewhat tongue in cheek, as letting: "you hand over your money to people you *do* trust, so they can look after them for your loved ones — and ideally keep things just boring enough that HMRC loses interest." In effect, you are still gifting your monies away as the **settlors** of a trust and the recipients of your largesse can still be your children, in the technical guise of '**beneficiaries** of the trust', except the *ownership* of the funds now resides with the trust and the timing, amounts and distribution of the trust's assets is dependent upon the discretion of **trustees** (of which you can be one, thus remaining in control). You could argue that a potential use of trusts is protecting the beneficiaries from themselves.

A good example of this can be illustrated by another of my clients named 'Grumpy Ian', who is aptly named, but not quite for the reasons you may think, especially the first time you meet this cheerful character and his ever-charming, endlessly patient wife, Sue. Now Ian owned a company that fitted burglar alarms and was something of a genius when it came to them; had he ever been asked to appear on *Mastermind* and chosen 'burglar alarms' as his specialist subject, it wouldn't have mattered if he then got every question in the general knowledge round wrong, for he would have secured so many points on burglar alarms that he would win each show by a huge margin.

He once demonstrated his expertise when I met up with them at a local pub one lunchtime to discuss what to do with the surplus cash within the company. It was a hot day and so we sat outside and as Grumpy Ian tucked into his pint and I sipped my sparkling water, he surveyed the houses across the road.

"See that one there, Lee," Ian would say, pointing to a large, well-appointed establishment. "Look at that alarm box – fake! You can tell by the way it's sitting on the wall. There's nothing behind it, just a shell. The owners there must think all burglars are stupid to do that! Mind you, look at the one next door – can you see the three wires coming from the bottom of it ?"

Squinting in the sunlight, I did my best.

"The thick wire in the middle is the electrical one, so I now know it runs off the mains. However the blue one next to it is the telephone wire that runs to the local nick, so you cut that one first then yank the leccy wire out and *voila*, you can go in."

"But what does the third one do?" I ventured, trying to show an interest.

"Decoy," responded Ian confidently. "It's there to throw burglars off the scent, but once you get to know these things …."

"I keep telling him he should become a master-criminal," trilled Sue. "Think how much more money we would have for you to invest, Lee, if Ian did that. This time next year, we'd be millionaires!"

"Na, Sue," responded Grumpy Ian. "I couldn't do that – it's not legit. That's why I like Lee – he's legit. Proper legit, not fancy legit like that other adviser we used to have – all fancy words, fancy reports and fancy promises. The only legit thing about him was his sky-high fees …" The conversation would then be interrupted by a phone call.

"Sorry Lee, gotta take this, business - one of the lads … Yeah …. no …. yeah … NO! What did we say in training the other day? Green to earth, brown to live, blue to ….. What do you mean you cannot find the blue wire? I'm starting to get grumpy now …."

So now you know why he's called Grumpy Ian.

His successful business meant both he and Sue had plenty of money and they wanted to help out their two boys, not least since they were now married with young children.

"He doesn't trust their wives," said Sue conspiratorially. "They like their designer gear, fancy holidays and fast cars – and Ian thinks that's where all the money will go. But I think well, why not, if that's what makes them happy. After all, we've got enough…."

"No, no, no, no, no, no, no," and just in case the message was in some way not clear enough, "Ab-So-Lute-Ly Not!" Grumpy Ian was not going to budge. However, he was definitely not grumpy about the solution I offered him – in fact he was over the moon.

What I proposed was the setting up of two **Discretionary Trusts** whereby £325,000 was gifted into one by Ian, while the same amount was gifted into the other by Sue. They were both named trustees along with a couple of their siblings for each trust, so were de facto still 'in control' of the money, while the beneficiaries were their two sons and their direct issue (children). **Letters of Wishes** were composed with the instructions that funds were only to be distributed to help with house purchases, weddings, university fees, etc … In doing this, Sue got her wish that funds had been passed to her two darling boys and Grumpy Ian's fears that it would be blown on fast cars and flash holidays were, somewhat, mollified and, provided they lived another seven years, £650,000 had been taken out of their estate.

However, before every reader rushes away to set up their own trusts, a few words of caution. A few paragraphs ago I mentioned that trusts were a Financial Adviser's best friend and an amateur investor's worst enemy, so they must be created with much due care, as well as, sometimes, expert legal advice, too. This is because HMRC does not wish to make it easy to avoid paying IHT, so there are many trip-wires haphazardly scattered throughout the journey to IHT nirvana designed to trap the unwary. For example, you will note that Grumpy Ian and Sue set up two identical trusts, rather than one and this is because if more than £325,000 is gifted into a Discretionary Trust, then an immediate IHT charge of 20% is liable on the excess (known as a **Chargeable Lifetime Transfer**), even though both these were two individuals gifting up to their nil rate IHT band at the same time, rather than one. Similarly, had the wrong type of trust been used, for example, an **Absolute Trust** rather than Discretionary, perhaps to 'cleverly' avoid the Chargeable Lifetime Transfer that is not levied on the former, then not only will the trustees not be able to subsequently vary when and how much the distributions could be made, but in the case of either of Ian and Sue's two boys getting divorced or getting into financial trouble, then the trust assets become fair game to insolvency practitioners and divorce lawyers, since both boys are 'absolutely' entitled to them, whereas with a discretionary trust, they are only entitled to what the trustees deem suitable, which could be as little as absolutely nothing. Furthermore, if trusts are not registered with HMRC, then they are liable to fines as well, whereas most disastrously of all, poorly timed Potential Exempt Transfers and setting-up of Discretionary Trusts could mean gifts made from as long ago as fourteen years before death being caught up in estates for any IHT calculations .....

Trusts therefore are complicated and should always be used as part of a long-term strategy that has been created and is cared for by an equally long-term, trusted Financial Adviser. The importance of the latter point can be demonstrated by a notorious case concerning a now wound-up firm of solicitors in Scotland who, mainly via extensive advertising especially on social media, heavily marketed a product called **Family Protection Trusts** that purported to be a solution to individuals who wished to avoid paying both Inheritance Tax, as well as potential Care Home fees (not to be confused with the similarly named, but very different, Protective Property Trusts of Chapter 4). So successful was their advertising that it was estimated at the time of writing in the summer of 2025, that they had sold over twenty-five thousand of these schemes, mainly to well-meaning people who thought they were doing the right thing, albeit acting on their own; in other words, the 'amateur DIY investor' I so warned about a couple of paragraphs ago.

Here is the issue. The firm 'selling' these things was a fully regulated, legitimate law firm, who purported to specialize in 'estate planning' – in other words, on the face of it, perfectly legitimate. However, the way this scheme works is to place a range of assets (property, savings, investments) into a trust *during the lifetime* of the settlor(s) for 'protection', while allowing them to continue being able to use them (such as the main residential home). If you were to ask any Financial Adviser what they thought of such an arrangement, each and every one of them would point out that this is what is known as a **Gift With Reservation of Benefit** (GWRB – see below) and, as such, would therefore fail to avoid having IHT levied upon the asset in consideration. Furthermore, placing an asset into trust (such as the family home) for no clear and obvious reason other than to avoid tax or Care Home fees would be challenged by local authorities, as they would view it as **deliberate deprivation of assets** (for the payment of Care Home fees). In other words, a Family Protection Trust fails to achieve what it promises to do and the reason why it fails is, frankly, very basic financial advice. In which case, you may not unreasonably ask, how did this firm get away with it ? The answer may be surprising – trusts (and wills) are not regulated; this means therefore that the maxim 'caveat emptor' (buyer beware) is more relevant than in some other areas of finance.

Setting up a trust is not the simplest thing to do, but it is hardly rocket science, so most decent Financial Advisers will probably charge around £250-£400 to do the work for you; this firm of solicitors were charging £3,000-£4,000, often more (N.B. a high setting-up fee for anything is usually a warning sign) and not only that, with the sheer volume of trusts they were writing, most weren't done properly either. Unfortunately, it gets even worse. The solicitors named themselves as sole trustees, probably in an attempt to justify their high charges – always an unnecessary thing to do, unless as an absolute last resort (i.e. the individuals have no suitable relatives or friends who could carry out the role) - and they also, for some reason, put a charge over the individuals' properties within the trust which, now the firm no longer exists, is proving to be a further nightmare, since these properties cannot be sold without the permission of a firm of solicitors that now doesn't exist. There's a saying many Financial Advisers are fond of quoting to their clients: "*If it sounds too good to be true, then it probably is*" and it would be wise to always pay heed to this, as well as what I said in the Introduction of this book that, "*Sadly, there is no silver bullet with regards to Inheritance Tax mitigation*". Unfortunately for far too many people, often elderly and vulnerable, this sorry saga of Family Protection Trusts was marketed as being just that 'silver bullet' which, indeed, proved too good to be true.

Stepping away from trusts, one structure that has gained significant attention in recent years is a **FICO**, or **Family Investment Company**, which can also be set up as a **Family Investment Limited Liability Partnership** (LLP), which we are going to examine now as an alternative vehicle to trusts for use with IHT planning.

In many ways, both of these structures have much in common with trusts, inasmuch they are all separate legal entities which are responsible for managing investments and distributing assets to nominated third parties, so why go to the bother of effectively setting up a whole company when a trust can effectively do the job in the first place? So let us drag Grumpy Ian, no doubt protesting loudly, as well as his poor, long-suffering wife Sue to illustrate why.

In their example above, both of them gifted £325,000 each into a Discretionary Trust, largely because that was the maximum allowed before triggering a Chargeable Lifetime Charge of 20% of the surplus over the IHT nil rate band. What this means is that had they instead gifted £3,250,000 into one of these trusts then there would have been an immediate tax charge as followed:

£3,250,000 (the gift)
less £325,000 (the IHT nil rate band)
= £2,925,000
@ 20%
= £585,000 in tax

At this point it doesn't need me to tell you what Grumpy Ian would have said about paying that amount of tax, even if it were permissible to publish his words in a publication like this. Instead, he and Sue could have set up Family Investment Co or LLP. For the purposes of this example, it is decided than an LLP will be incorporated with Ian, Sue, their two boys and four grandchildren as members (since the grandchildren are under the age of eighteen, their membership is held for them by their parents). Grumpy Ian and Sue inject £3,250,000 as start-up capital, simultaneously instructing their accountant to credit the capital as [£3,250,000/4 =] £812,500 each to themselves and their two boys, which effectively means a Potentially Exempt Transfer of £812,500 to each of their two lads. Like a trust deed, they set up an LLP Agreement which stipulates that Ian and Sue can outvote all the other members on all the important issues related to the operation of the LLP, which would include any purchase and sale of investments, the annual allocation of investment income, as well as, critically, the ability to withdraw capital from the LLP by any member. In other words, it is just like a trust inasmuch that the funds are still under the control of Ian and Sue with income and capital being able to be allocated when and to whom at their discretion except, crucially, there is no upfront chargeable lifetime 20% IHT charge. Moreover, income distributed from a Discretionary Trust comes heavily taxed with a tax credit which the recipient needs to claim back, whereas any income distribution from a Family Income LLP is taxed at their marginal rate of the receiving member via their self-assessment tax returns.

In several respects, FICOs and Family Investment LLPs are superb alternatives to trusts especially for larger sums of money, which can therefore sidestep the 20% Chargeable Lifetime Transfer. That said, at present, their comparative rarity means that the necessary work on the part of accountants does come with a hefty price-tag that can only be justified by bigger sums of money involved, plus anything other than cash (i.e. existing investments, property etc) will almost certainly result in Capital Gains Tax being levied on the transfer of ownership.

Family Investment LLPs and FICOs are probably the ideal solutions for large gifts that would potentially be heavily taxed by using a Discretionary Trust. However, even they cannot address the thorny issue of the principal private residence.

It is quite understandable that people faced with their largest asset (i.e. their Principal Private Residence) should wish to somehow save as much of its value as possible so to bequeath it to their children. If you ask any Financial Adviser, they will tell you that at least several times a year they are asked by someone if they can avoid paying IHT by gifting their main residence to their children and then continuing to live in it which, as the saga of the Family Protection Trust above proves, just does not work as HMRC would view this as a Gift With Reservation of Benefit. It doesn't have to be property that fails this test – if an individual owns a painting that is valued at several million pounds, then 'gifts' the ownership of it to one of their children but keeps the thing hanging on the wall over his fireplace, in other words continuing to enjoy the 'beneficial ownership' than HMRC would merely point out that the 'gifting' did not really occur and so would expect the value of the painting to be included in any calculation to establish if any IHT was true.

There is an exception to this, and this is when the individual making the gift then pays the full market rate for hiring it back – however, it is fraught with challenges and pitfalls as the following sorry tale demonstrates.

Debbie Denmark has to be one of my kindest clients, especially so if you happened to be a cat, since every stray one within a ten-mile radius of her home knew Debbie as the ultimate feline foster mother, always welcoming every Tom, Tigger and Whiskers with a saucer of fresh milk and, if so needed, a basket and blanket for the night. Her poor, long-suffering husband had the indignity of being nicknamed 'Colin the Cat' by his staff since he was allergic to them, but he stoically soldiered on, as the devoted and supporting partner of Debbie and put up with the seemingly never-ending cat invasion. I, too, have been nicknamed 'The Cat' as part of my dark and murky past, on that occasion in honour of the great Russian goalkeeper Lev Yashin, a.k.a. The Black Cat, when I played in goal for my local work team and proved to be as much use as a stuffed Garfield the cat toy; however, I am also allergic to them too, so whenever I visited London Colney's unofficial cattery, Colin and I would be sitting around the table with our eyes streaming and sneezing away, as Debbie would coo over her latest rescued moggy.

I had been referred to Debbie and Colin by their accountant, a rather dark and wily operator, as in his words: "They have just inherited a load of money and so now for some reason they have given me loads of billable work to do, since they have to pay a load of Income Tax, as well as Capital Gains on it." Now, hopefully by this stage in the book, you, fair reader, would understand that it is Inheritance Tax that is payable on death, not Income Tax or Capital Gains tax and while the accountant may well have been a shady character, he was not stupid, so I was intrigued and offered to help. Unfortunately, the story I encountered was a very sad one, another that demonstrates the folly of people acting upon their own initiative and with the best of intentions, but with catastrophic consequences.

What happened occurred to Debbie's mum and dad, Elizabeth and Philip, who never considered themselves wealthy at all, but owned a house that was sufficient in value to put the estate of the second one of them to die, over the IHT nil-rate threshold. A good dozen years or so before they died, they had realised this, so formally gifted the ownership of their beautiful home to their daughter, Debbie, whose accountant warned them, quite correctly, that the parents would need to pay a rent to Debbie or else HMRC would consider it a Gift with Reservation. Speaking to a local estate agent, they were advised that a rent of £3,000 a month would fairly reflect the current market value, that Elizabeth and Philip were easily able to pay out of their pensions, which Debbie then reported to her accountant as one of her various sources of income. Eventually, both of Debbie's parents died peacefully of old age, but before she had time to grieve properly, HMRC came along and started asking some rather pointed questions about this set up involving her late parents' home and so sent their district valuer round to investigate. They concluded that the true market rental for the property at the time of Debbie's parents death was actually £4,000 a month, which meant that the actual rent paid was less than the full market rate which meant, to everyone's horror, HMRC then judged that the transfer of the house to Debbie was a Gift With Reservation of Benefit, since Elizabeth and Philip had been living there at a rent that was less than that of the going rate of the market, meaning they continued to enjoy the benefit of an asset that had been 'given away.' Unfortunately, the rules surrounding anti-avoidance of any kind of tax, not least gifting to avoid IHT, are, perhaps through necessity, extremely rigid and so the whole of Debbie's parents' property was returned to the estate to be assessed for IHT. Furthermore, Debbie had naturally been paying income tax on the rent received for all the years the arrangements were in place and when the house was eventually sold, Capital Gains Tax was liable on the increase in value from when the house was originally gifted some dozen or so years, since the house was now in Debbie's name, not her parents who would have benefited from Capital Gains tax main residence relief, a triple-tax whammy, if ever there was one.

There is, however, an almost happy ending to this story. Alongside Debbie's accountant, I argued that the intention of the above was never to defraud HMRC and therefore that the taxman should not benefit from an arrangement that effectively gives them "free gifts" of Income and Capital Gains tax, in addition to Inheritance Tax and, to their credit, they have agreed, even if no refund of tax has yet been authorised at the time of writing this book. So, to find out if Debbie's accountant and I were successful, you will just have to buy the sequel to this book to find out whodunnit.

In summary then, my mantra that IHT planning is a journey that does not have a silver bullet solution is once more being repeated, with the addition that the use of gifting and trusts can certainly play a part on this journey. The rules change, valuations fluctuate and people's circumstances alter, so it is a journey that needs to be planned, regularly reviewed by a trusted Financial Adviser and put together in such a way that it bends in the wind, because the only thing that can be guaranteed would indeed be the winds of change.

CHAPTER 7

Old Macdonald had a Farm (Agricultural and Business relief)

'Ah, Inheritance Tax, Minister: the ingenious system whereby the Treasury ensures that a citizen's patriotic duty to fund the state does not end merely because they've stopped breathing' — Sir Humphrey Appleby, *Yes Minister,* BBC TV

In the Autumn of 2024 and after weeks of speculation, Rachel Reeves delivered her first budget as Chancellor of the Exchequer of the new Labour government desperate to raise additional funding through taxation. Hedged in by pre-election promises by her colleagues not to raise Income Tax or National Insurance, as well as the previous Conservative administration who had raided Capital Gains Tax to such an extent that there was hardly anything left worth changing, she instead turned her attention to the only one tax remaining: Inheritance Tax. The changes proposed were drastic and controversial, with hardly anyone outside of the Labour Party thinking they were remotely good ideas; in short, death values of personal pensions would be once again subject to IHT, while Business Property and Agricultural Relief would be significantly cut. This chapter aims to explain what these Reliefs aimed to do, how they work, what qualifies and what changes have been proposed.

Business Property Relief (BPR – now commonly abbreviated to **Business Relief)** has sometimes been described as the government's way of saying "thanks for running a business" — by letting some business assets slip past Inheritance Tax (IHT) calculations, or at least be much less bitey. What it aims to do when someone dies, is to reduce the value of certain business assets for IHT purposes by either 100% or 50%, meaning those assets can be exempt (or half-exempt) from individuals' estates if they meet certain conditions. You usually need to have owned the qualifying business property for at least two years before death for BPR to apply and it aims to protect trading businesses and family farms from being forced into a fire sale to pay IHT — the original intention was to keep businesses running rather than breaking them up to raise cash.

What kinds of assets qualify? (and what don't)

Typically eligible (Relevant Business Property):

A sole trader's business or partnership interests.

- Shares in an unlisted company (or in some "not listed" categories).
- Certain business assets used in the business (plant, machinery, goodwill, land/ buildings used by the business).

Common exclusions:

- Investment assets (simply holding stocks for investment) usually won't qualify.
- If a company is mainly an investment company rather than a trading company, BPR may not apply.
- Shares quoted on the main market may not get 100% relief; some listed markets and AIM shares have special treatment, but the rules are changing (see below).

Rates, timing and the "two-year" rule

- **100% relief** commonly applies to full trading assets and qualifying unlisted shares.
- **50% relief** applies to some assets that are less purely trading.
- **Ownership test:** The deceased must generally have owned the asset for 2 years before death.

As an example, Mrs Patel owns a neighbourhood bakery (a proper trading business) that is valued at £650,000. On her death, the bakery could get 100% BPR so its value is ignored for IHT — provided the conditions are met and she has owned it for two years.

Similarly, if she retired at 60 and handed the reins to her daughter who continued the family business, Mrs Patel would still be entitled to full relief – you do not need to be actively involved in the day-to-day running of the enterprise to qualify for the relief. However, if she instead handed over the business to her son, who was unwilling to contemplate the early starts and hard graft, so instead rented the business premises to another entity, then Mrs Patel would lose the relief since it is no longer a *trading* company, but instead and *investment* (ie rental) one.

Mention must be made here of investments, explored further within the next chapter, which invest in shares of these types of companies. As the previous point makes clear, an individual does not need to be working within the company to be entitled to the relief, so it is quite possible to invest in portfolios that are made up of shares that have invested in a number of different companies, all of which are entitled to Business Property Relief. Often these types of investments are called **AIM Investments** since they are shares in smaller companies listed on the Alternative Investment Market, a subsidiary of the main London Stock Exchange, but there are others that are unlisted that still qualify for the relief through the nature of their trading activities.

Agricultural Relief works in pretty much the same way, with the exception that recognition is given that the main private residence which is nearly always located within the middle of a farm, so that is included in the assets exempt from IHT as well.

In the Autumn Budget 2024, the Chancellor of the Exchequer, Rachel Reeves, announced reforms to BPR and Agricultural Property Relief (APR) which take effect from April 6, 2026. These are the key points:

1. **A combined cap:** The highest rate of relief (100%) will apply only to the first £1 million of combined business and agricultural property per taxpayer (on top of the existing nil-rate band) [*In the Autumn Budget of November 2025, the Chancellor of the Exchequer, Ms Reeves, confirmed that this allowance could be transferred in its entirety on first death to spouse's of married couples, as well as partners in civil partnerships meaning, in those circumstances, £2 million of relief would be available. This was extended further the following month to £2.5 million per person*, producing a maximum potential nil rate of £5,650,000 for couples/civil partners, that would include the IHT nil rate, but not the RNRB since the estate in this example would be over £2.7 million.]*

2. **Reduced rate above £2.5 million*:** Any value above £1 million will be eligible for 50% relief rather than 100%.

3. **AIM shares:** Relief for AIM shares will be reduced to 50% in all circumstances. Unlisted investments that qualify for business relief (BR) will be able to mitigate the

full 40% IHT charge up to a £1m threshold, but after that point, a 20% tax rate will be levied* (at the time of writing this book in the summer of 2025, it is rumoured that the Treasury is strongly considering bringing those unlisted investments in line with [listed] AIM shares).

4. **Payment flexibility for estates:** For IHT due because of these changes, the government introduced the ability to pay over time — interest-free instalments over up to 10 years for qualifying cases.

If we take Mrs Patel's bakery above since its value is £650,000, under the new rules it's still within the £2.5m* cap, so it should continue to enjoy 100% relief (i.e., effectively no IHT on that asset). However, if it was valued at £3,125,000 then the first £2,500,000 would continue to enjoy 100% relief, while the remaining £650,000 would be assessed to IHT as followed:

£650,000
@ 40% (the rate of IHT)
= £260,000
@ 50% (the new relief)
= **£130,000 tax liable**

This book is not intended to pass commentary upon the wisdom of politicians – it would be a rather short one if it was. Instead, it aims to educate and inform, thus enabling the reader to make informed judgements and decisions, so the idea of Ms Reeves' reforms was to focus on individuals who have made small fortunes, for example in running investment funds in the City, or by presenting successful television shows about fast cars, who used their newly-made fortunes to retire and buy farms in the idyllic British countryside, to live in the beautiful farmhouses on the land, while employing genuine farmers to run the business, all the while benefitting from having the farmland and main residence exempt from IHT. It is a well-trodden strategy for Inheritance Tax mitigation with much documented information on how to 'persuade' HMRC that you are running a legitimate business, rather than attempting to avoid paying Inheritance Tax by merely having a luxurious mansion that just happens to be on a farm. Whether Ms Reeves' attempt to snare this type of activity to bring some of the wealth back to the public purse, is using the proverbial sledgehammer to crack a nut with significant collateral of catching other, far less wealthy, genuine family farming businesses in the net too, is up to you to decide. What it does prove conclusively, is how things are constantly changing in the world of financial planning and therefore the importance of having a long-term, trusted individual working alongside you to ensure that when changes do occur, your own financial plan is adjusted accordingly.

CHAPTER 8

Policy & Prejudice (Life Assurance, equity release & tax efficient investments)

'Only the British could turn dying into a taxable event' – Anon

I first met Russell and Wendy in those strange times in early 2020. They were strange since we all knew that year during January and February, that something unusual was happening in China, a disease which was apparently killing people on a terrifying scale, a disease which soon turned up on the shores of the United Kingdom, forcing the country in lockdowns: Covid. Little could we foresee such events when I first met this charming couple one evening late in February 2020, nor that as a result Ralph would lose his job (much to his delight) in the high-end jewellery industry when rich foreign tourists stopped visiting the UK. Their lives were turned upside down, so every Thursday at 7pm we spoke about the sudden need for early retirement for an hour on speakerphone (since they were terrible with the internet, so Zoom was out of the question) which always ended just before eight o'clock, so we could all go out onto our doorsteps and clap the NHS workers who bravely kept the country on its feet during those troubled times.

But this is not a story about Russell and Wendy, who lived in a wonderful house in Woking which belonged to Russell's father, General Ralph. Now The General was a remarkable man and the first time I met him, he was splendidly decked out in his uniform and medals all ready to be taken to a military union, which in response to my genuinely interested query, was Burma.

"What, 1941-1945 ? " I asked, incredulously.
"Yes, that's right young man," answered the General, with what I hoped was an element of being impressed.
"But…." I stammered.
"Yes," said Russell, reading my mind, "He's ninety-five years old !"

Now there may well have been a good reason for my confusion, since The General had just come back from walking the dog and I had been told he played bridge online, every night, over the internet whose mysterious workings still elude both Russell and Wendy to this day. Indeed, it is a routine which is still being followed some five years later when writing this book, as he rapidly approaches the moment when he gets a birthday card from the King, even if he still hasn't disclosed to me the secret of eternal life. These days, The General spends his time in the grandpa-annex to his home, like a good-natured and benevolent silverback gorilla who likes nothing more than handing over the reins of the day-to-day running of his troop to someone else, while instead he has fun letting his great grandchildren climb all over him whenever they came to visit.

As befitting a retired King of the Jungle, General Ralph had also enjoyed a successful career in industry and now, with a generous pension and plenty of savings, his son was becoming increasingly worried that The General had not made any provision towards planning for any IHT for which his estate would almost certainly be liable. However, like so many people in this situation, discussions about impending mortality were not easy to initiate, so they did not happen. Instead, I was gradually introduced over many months, that turned into years, until this great, retired silverback finally decided he could trust me; and then we set to work.

As I have repeatedly stated in this book, IHT planning is a journey, so the sooner you get to the starting line and the earlier you start implementing the recommendations of any plan, the better the potential outcomes could be. At the grand old age of 98 years old, The General had decided to start his final campaign rather late in the day and a cynic may have observed that the battle was largely over, with HMRC having taken over positions in the battlefield that were, on the face of it, somewhat unassailable. In some respects, this is true – any substantial gift now had the added jeopardy that the donor is more unlikely than not to be around to see the end of the requisite seven-year waiting period on his one hundred and fifth birthday. However, there are still things that can be done as hinted at in the previous chapter, specifically regular gifting out of surplus income, as well as consideration to investing in investments[(See Note 3)] that attract Business Property Relief.

This is exactly what we did for The General. Not with all of his savings, not with all of his assets and not with the outcome of reducing his potential IHT liability completely, but at least some of his *surplus* assets would now be removed from his estate for IHT purposes if The General lived the required two years after making the investment.

Now, these type of investments are considered high-risk, usually since they are granted to shares in companies that are small, in niche and growing industries that the government wishes to encourage growth in. One area the government is currently keen to direct investment is into companies that buy and then lease expensive equipment to hospitals with the result that when a hospital requires the use of a hugely expensive machine that would ordinarily be used only occasionally, instead of having to pay for the cost of buying one, as well as its ongoing storage and maintenance, they instead lease the machine from one of these third-party companies. For many years, companies involved in the manufacturing of solar panels also attracted BPR on their shares – until the government one day decided to just withdraw that concession. This is one of the reasons these type of investments are deemed 'high risk', since things can change very quickly at the whim of a politician, as well as market forces. Indeed, The General also suffered somewhat in this regard, when Rachel Reeves announced in her budget of 2024 changes to BPR on these type of investments, as discussed in the previous chapter. Of course, you could argue that paying 20% of something is better than 40%, but it just goes to reinforce the message of ongoing planning, not least since the only way to get the relief is to have held the assets for at least two years and, crucially, to still own them upon death.

One strategy The General could have followed, had he been a little younger when he started his IHT planning journey, would be to pay for a Whole of Life Insurance policy[See Note 4] from his surplus income. This is effectively a life assurance policy with a guaranteed payout since the whole of an individual's life inevitably ends with meeting their Maker. It is written in trust, with nominated beneficiaries, meaning that on death the benefits by-pass probate as well as IHT, which could be very useful when looking to pay an IHT liability to release probate. It is a curious fact that insurance companies like the idea of a regular income in the form of monthly premiums, which they can in turn invest themselves to make a profit, meaning that in some cases the eventual payout is higher than the premiums paid into the plan. As always with these things, careful planning and research needs to be undertaken even if, unfortunately, in the case of The General, he was too old when he became my client for any company to have any inclination to insure him.

We are going to revisit this kind of strategy again later on in this chapter, but first I want to introduce to you another client of mine named Minnie Prime and her two charming daughters, Joyce and Delma who between them formed a terrific trio in life; after nearly every one of my regular visits to them, I would be returning to my car chuckling to myself at their antics, since they certainly knew how to live life to the full. That said, I always had the greatest admiration for Minnie who, after a career as a NHS nurse (not an easy gig by any stretch of the imagination), retired at sixty and instead of hanging up her stethoscope and thermometer, used her pension tax free lump sum and savings to set up a Care Home for adults who needed a little bit of support in navigating Life. For many years, whenever I visited one of them, they would be exhausted from their work but their burning commitment and heartfelt care towards their residents was something you could not but greatly admire. Eventually, though, Minnie decided that even she should retire and so sold the Care Home for a fair few millions of pounds in profit, which now made her not only quite wealthy, but also with a sizeable potential IHT liability.

One of the first things she did, at my instigation, was to treat herself to a holiday and it was agreed that, on her return, all three of us would meet up to start planning the way forward for not just Minnie, but the girls too, who had also benefited from the sale of the home.

Now for some reason, we always met at Joyce's house, perhaps because she liked to entertain and so fussed around us all like an extremely attentive Mother Hen cooing affectionately at her brood. Eventually, once she was happy that we had enough food and drink to survive the next hour, she sat down and announced:

"You will never guess what Mummy has gone and done?"

"She hasn't gone and bought another Care Home?" I responded, somewhat tongue in cheek.

"Noooo – well I hope not!"

Minnie shook her head.

"On her holiday, that 'cruise' around the Med which *you* encouraged her to take. Well, she ordered a limo to pick her up from her house to take her to the docks at Southampton, where she got aboard, went to her room, jumped into bed and watched TV there for three weeks, never once leaving her room. Everything was room service, she didn't set foot onto the gangway outside her cabin, let alone on land at any of the countries the ship docked at…."

"Oh, I had such a wonderful time," chuckled Minnie.

"You could have come to my house and spent all day in bed watching TV," fulminated Delma. "I would have waited on you hand and foot for the fraction of the cost of that cruise!"

"No, no, no, no," laughed Minnie. "It was so nice and peaceful!"

The girls were, perhaps understandably, outraged – but Minnie was strangely content, so instead attention was turned to the Financial Adviser who had, with the best of intentions, told Minnie that she should be spending money on herself now she has properly retired.

"What do you think of my cake then?" asked Joyce, nodding towards the untouched slice on my plate.

"Um, very ni ….." I had barely got the words out, before Delma interrupted.

"You're not feeding him your Rum Cake, are you, Joyce? You know, Lee is tee-total and doesn't drink, so what are you thinking?"

"He's not drinking it, sister – he's eating it, so that doesn't count!"

"Of course it does, you silly moo – especially with the amount of rum you pour into them!"

"Oh, I like my rum!" chuckled Minnie.

"See," Joyce, responded triumphantly. "Mummy likes it, so it must be good. Anyway, I only add a little bit of extra rum and everyone always comments on how flavoursome my cakes are."

"They're flippin' fire hazards, if you ask me. There's more rum in one of your cakes than the entire Caribbean!"

"You are being nasty now, sister. Anyway, if you didn't like my rum cakes, why are you always taking some home with you ?"

"For my barbeques," answered Delma, innocently fluttering her eyelashes.

"Hmm," Joyce responded thoughtfully. "I suppose it would taste nice toasted with a hint of smoke …"

"No, I don't eat them. I use them to *light* my barbeques – they're very good in that regard."

"You set fire to my cakes?"

"They go up like an inferno …."

In between cakes, cruises, rum, blazing barbeques and equally blazing rows, sometimes some financial planning did actually get done with Minnie and her two daughters. In particular, special attention was given to Minnie's pressing problem of having now accumulated an impressive amount of wealth that was now in danger of being eroded by a potential IHT bill upon her death. So what we did was to establish how much income Minnie really wanted for her retirement (by using the budget planner in the next chapter), looked at what she was receiving already from her NHS and State pensions, worked out the shortfall and set to work.

One of the types of policies we decided to use was what is called a **Gift and Loan Plan**. This involved Minnie setting up a trust, by first gifting it a small amount (usually something like £1 or £5) to start it, following this up with an interest-free loan to the trust, repayable on demand (which allows Minnie to retain access to the capital, if needed), but usually over a period of twenty years. This is because the loan is then usually invested in what is known as an Investment Bond, which allows the donor to withdraw up to 5% or the original investment each policy* year (* the date the policy was set up, not calendar or tax year) without an immediate Income Tax or Capital Gains Tax charge, as it is deemed to be a return of capital, or in this case, the repayment of the loan. The repayment term is therefore 20 years, since the withdrawals are 5%, but it could be made longer if appropriate by taking lower withdrawal amounts. For IHT purposes, the loan remains part of the estate but, of course, as each year passes, it diminishes in value, whereas any growth on the Investment Bond remains outside of the estate. At the time of writing this book, Minnie had set the plan up just over nine years ago, so [9 x 5% =] 45% of the original loan is now outside of her estate, as is all the growth from the investment, while she has used her enhanced monthly income wisely to enjoy further cruises and, not so wisely, by investing in Joyce's cake-making company. So if one day, you happen to be visiting Watford and hear a loud explosion followed by a pungent smell of rum, now you know what will have caused it.

An alternative to the above for Minnie, could have been **Discounted Gift Plan**, which works in a very similar fashion, once more having a donor place a sum of money into a trust which, once again invests into an Investment Bond, thereby allowing a 5% return of capital, in the form of income. The key difference though is that under a Gift and Loan Plan, the donor can recall the money at any time, whereas with a Discounted Plan they cannot – it is an irreversible gift, or a PET (potentially exempt transfer), which therefore falls out of the estate for IHT purposes if Minnie were to survive seven years or more. Likewise, the income in a Discounted Gift Plan is an entitlement for the rest of donor's life, which also has a measurable actuarial value based on the donor's age, health, and withdrawal level- and it is only this that stays in Minnie's estate, even though she is receiving income based upon the whole initial value of the gift. This is a tricky plan to understand, so here is a worked example with our friend Minnie that *might* make things clearer:

- Donor: Minnie who is aged 70 and in good health.
- Lump sum invested into the plan: £500,000.
- Regular withdrawals retained: £25,000 per year (5% of initial investment).
- Trust type: Discretionary trust.
- Minnie survives more than 7 years from the gift.

Step 1 – Actuarial "discount"

When the plan is set up, an actuary values the Minnie's lifetime right to withdrawals. For a healthy 70-year-old taking £25,000 p.a., this discount might be valued at £150,000. That £150,000 is the actuarial estimate of the benefit the donor has kept for life, so it is not treated as a gift for IHT purposes — it stays in the donor's estate.

Step 2 – The gift portion

The remainder of the investment is treated as the lifetime gift, as calculated below:

£500,000 total investment.
minus £150,000 (the retained benefit [discount])
= £350,000 which then becomes a PET

If the donor survives 7 years, then the Potentially Exempt Transfer (PET) of £350,000 is fully outside their estate.

Step 3 – IHT outcome comparison

Situation at Death	Impact on Estate	IHT @ 40%
No DGP (full £500k still in Estate)	£500,000	£200,000
With DGP, die within 7 years	£150,000 + £350,000 PET (less any taper relief)	Up to £200,000 but reduced because PET is only £350,000
With DGP, survive 7 years	£150,000 (discounted portion only)	£60,000

Step 4 – Key effect

- **Immediate reduction**: The actuarial discount (£150,000) is outside the gift calculation from day one.
- **Potential long-term removal**: Surviving 7 years removes the £350,000 PET from Minnie's estate.
- **Growth advantage**: Any growth on the gifted portion inside the trust is also outside the estate.

Sometimes when you are reading financial articles, you may stumble across jargon that you don't understand. In the past some Financial Advisers used to pride themselves on being able to bamboozle people with their seemingly brilliant knowledge masked by impenetrable language, something that the industry has done its best to eradicate in recent years. However, you may still come across the terms *liquid* and *illiquid* to describe certain assets – a liquid asset is not something to do with water or oil, but is rather something that can be accessed easily, such as cash, than can be 'liquidated' quickly from a bank account; conversely, property is illiquid, since it is difficult to access as it is usually in the form of a large, cumbersome unit that takes ages to sell. With many people, this illiquid asset is their main residence.

One of the strangest challenges facing the retired today is that they are often asset rich, but cash poor, which usually means the house they own and live in, their main residence, has significant value, but their pension income is often meagre. A typical solution to this has often involved 'unlocking' the value of a person's main residence using what is known as **Equity Release**(See Note 5).

Equity release allows homeowners (usually over 55) to borrow money against the value of their home. The loan and any interest is rolled up and usually repaid from the estate after death, rather than by monthly repayments and while, in the past, there have been horror stories about properties used being plunged into negative equity (i.e. having a debt that is greater than the value of the property itself), as well as with children outraged that their inheritances have been wiped out, the industry has since introduced safeguards to ensure these unfortunate scenarios no longer happen.

Retirement Interest-Only Mortgages are very similar, again allowing homeowners to borrow money against the value of their home; this time however, only the interest is paid monthly to the lender, usually out of pension income, if that is affordable. What both schemes enable to happen is to release significant wealth from otherwise illiquid assets that can be passed down to children during an individual's lifetime. However, both also can be very effective in IHT planning, too.

For example, Toni and Rosina's total estate is worth £1.3 million, which after both of their IHT Nil Rate band (£325,000) and Residence Nil Rate Band (£175,000) has been used, means anything over [2 x (£325,000 + £175,0000 =] £1,000,000 is subject to the 40% tax charge, which in their case would be [£300,000 @ 40% =] £120,000. However, if they had taken out either an Equity Release or Retirement Interest-Only Mortgage for £300,000, then their net estate would then only be £1,000,000 meaning there would be no tax to pay. Clearly though, they would be well advised to gift or spend the funds released by the mortgage, or else the whole exercise would fail, since all they would have done is to move £300,000 from one asset (i.e. their main residence) and put it somewhere else (i.e. their bank account).

Working with a Financial Adviser can sometimes produce plans that become greater than the sum of their parts. I have seen Retirement Interest-Only mortgages used to release funds from a main residence, which has then been placed within a Discounted Gift Plan with the resulting income then being used as regular expenditure to not just pay the mortgage, but also funding a Whole of Life insurance plan written in trust, that collectively increases the overall legacy being left to the children. At the end of the day, it all depends upon what you want and how you have put together your plan to achieve this and it is precisely this that will be examined in the next chapter.

CHAPTER 9

One Plan to Rule them All
(Putting everything together)

"One Plan to rule them all, One Adviser to guide them,
Lasting Powers of Attorney, in case of falls
and a proper Will to bind them."
(based upon '*The Lord of the Rings*' by JRR Tolkien)

"A journey of a thousand miles begins with a single step" – Lao Tzu, ancient Chinese philosopher and author of 'The Tao Te Ching'

It should be no surprise to the reader at this point of the text to read my oft-uttered-to-clients mantra, that '*Inheritance Tax planning is a journey, not a one-stop fix-all event*', although it is to be hoped that by now this journey is not as dauting for you as the one Frodo Baggins had to undertake when he returned The Ring to the fires of Mount Doom, as paraphrased at the header of this chapter. Similarly, it is recommended that it is a journey undertaken alongside a wise guide, usually a trusted Financial Adviser who perhaps had helped you retire and may now guide you once more throughout retirement.

However, once you have decided to undertake this journey, you should be very wary of the temptation to procrastinate - procrastination is not just the thief of time, but in, IHT planning, can end up costing your estate a lot of money as well. It's never too early to begin planning, putting together a strategy that fits your own hopes in retirement, alongside what you want to leave as a lasting legacy to your family. So what follows in this chapter are a number of steps which aim to guide the reader on such a journey, whether they decide to do it with a Financial Adviser, or on their own.

Start with a Conversation: In the first instance, talking to your nearest and dearest is always a good start. This is never an easy conversation since nobody wants to talk to you about what might happen when you die and it may also be the case that some may not agree with your plans either – but at least you now know this. Conversations about passing on wealth will always raise a lot of questions — practical and emotional. You may have dependent persons who may need help and support from other family members once you have gone, or you may be worried about your children getting married or divorced, with the financial implications that could have on the family wealth. Maybe one of your children is encountering challenges in their lives that nobody had anticipated, so you want to put in place some controls over the wealth they receive, or there might be a family business that you wish to protect. Perhaps even you want your wealth to benefit charitable organisations to create a legacy after you're gone. All this needs to be talked about with both professionals and family.

Drafting a Will: In Chapter 5 it was noted that just over fifty percent of adults in the United Kingdom have a will; that means it is highly likely that one in two people reading this now therefore won't have one – just make sure it isn't you. Passing on wealth is about helping to ensure it goes to the right people in the right way, whether that's family and loved ones, or charitable causes close to your heart. This is the function of a will, the second step on your journey.

Lasting Powers of Attorney: A Lasting Power of Attorney (LPA) is a legal document which enables a named individual(s), the Attorney(s), to act on behalf of an individual in a legal capacity. There are two types, specifically one for finance, as well as another for health and welfare and they are especially useful for elderly parents, in particular those who may be frail or have dementia; however, do note that only someone of sound state of mind can grant an attorney, which often means it is too late to set one up at a time when they are particularly needed. I have had clients with active LPAs in their forties – you never know what life has in store for you, so having these set up and stored somewhere safely (usually with your Financial Adviser) is prudent financial planning. There is no point in making numerous plans to safeguard your wealth from unnecessary IHT, if this wealth is then managed by the Court of Protection in your later years, which is what would happen if there are no LPAs in place. Usually, LPAs are drafted the same time as a Will; both need to be stored somewhere safely and most decent Financial Advisers will offer you the facility for this to happen for, after all, they are the one person on the planet who ought to know about all your worldly goods, what you want to happen to them when you die and how to access them when such a sad event happens; after all, what are you paying them for?

Emergency Funds & Care Home fees: One of the greatest fears of individuals growing old is the prospect of all the wealth they had accumulated during their lifetime being eroded by Care Home fees. It is an understandable, as well as perfectly rational concern to have, especially with the eye-watering costs involved. However, the reality actually surprises many people; a survey undertaken by *BUPA* in 2019 established that the actual time spent in Care Homes is far shorter than most people imagine with 43% staying in one for less than a year and 30% staying one to three years, with only the remainder being in one for longer, usually because they had become very ill at a young age. What this means in the context of planning is that three years of net potential Care Home costs should be set aside, just in case. With our friend The General in Chapter 8, we established that the cost of Care Home fees were £700-£800 a week in 2025 (according to the NHS - www.nhs.uk/social-care-and-support/money-work-and-benefits/paying-for-your-own-care-self-funding) which equates to £41,600 a year, but he wanted a Care Home close to where he lived in expensive, leafy Surrey with would be £70,000 a year. Since his pension income was £50,000 a year, we worked out that he therefore needed an extra £20,000 a year for three years, therefore set aside [3 x £20,000 =] £60,000 for these fees. He also had one year's worth of income at £50,000 in cash for 'emergency funds' just in case he needed to do urgent work on his house. This is prudent financial planning, giving people peace of mind in the worst case scenarios and is the fourth step on the planning journey – there's no point in giving away large portions of your wealth if you then need to ask to have it back.

Bucket Lists: Retirement is often referred to as the final act of a person's life, so if that is the case you owe to yourself to make sure it's fun. Everyone should have a bucket list and while it doesn't mean to say you need to be jumping out of aeroplanes, or scuba diving with Great White Sharks (unless you want to of course), slightly less adrenaline-fueled activities such as taking the whole family and grandchildren to *Disneyland* is just as viable a goal. Either way, whatever they are, make a note of them, put a cost on them and start looking forward to when they will happen. I often find that this fifth step is the most fun.

Work out your spending needs: Everybody hates completing budget planners – and I hate nagging my clients to complete them too; however, it is mission critical in any form of financial planning to establish how much it costs to lead the lifestyle you do and how it is going to be funded.

This is probably a cue for the entire readership to groan as I now encourage them to complete the Budget Planner on the next page of this book, but the brutal message is that you don't want to run out of money in retirement, unless you want to go back out to work again. In short, this is for your financial security, therefore is of super-importance, so it is at this point that I would introduce once again one of my favourite pastimes which is *Cashflow Modelling.*

ANTICIPATED MONTHLY EXPENDITURE	CURRENT EXPENDITURE	DESIRED RETIREMENT EXPENDITURE
Anticipated mortgage payment (if applicable)		
Shared ownership/rent (if applicable)		
Property insurance		
Contents insurance		
Ground rent/service charge (leasehold property only)		
Property repairs/decoration		
Council Tax		
Electricity		
Gas/oil		
Water rates		
Telephone/mobile costs		
TV rental/licence/Sky TV		
Healthcare costs (i.e. glasses/hearing aids/ad hoc procedures, etc)		
Housekeeping/food		
Clothing/hairdressing		
Car loan/personal loan/HP		
Credit cards		
Public transport costs/petrol		
Car repairs/servicing/tax/insurance/ AA etc...		
Holidays		
Entertainment/hobbies		
Contribution to school fees/college fees		

Grandchildren's treats/pocket money/birthday and Christmas presents		
Pet costs/vet bills/insurance		
Charitable giving		
Anything else		
TOTAL		

A Cashflow Model: It is quite possible that many people reading this book already have a Financial Adviser and, if you are lucky, they may be one of the few who actively uses a Cashflow Model with them as part of their financial planning; my challenge to those individuals who have Financial Advisers who do not, would be this: what exactly are you ,paying for then?

For once you have established what income you will need to support your lifestyle in retirement, how much you need for emergency funds and potential Care Home fees, as well as plotting planned bucket list events, you then need to link it all to your various income streams and investments/assets; in short, are your funds going to last you for the rest of your life and, if so, how much is going to be left over and what is the likely IHT bill be at this point. It will therefore not be a surprise to you that a decent Cashflow Model can apply a scientific approach to this question, incorporating various 'what if' scenarios such as dying earlier than expected and how much may any potential IHT bill be at that point. In short, it is only at the sixth step of planning that you start to consider the thorny issue of tax.

Establish Surplus and what you want to happen to it: At this point, you should now have the peace of mind of knowing your money is not going to run out, you can afford all the things you want to do in retirement, that if you need to go into Care the funds have been set aside, as well as when you die a properly drafted Will means that your remaining wealth is distributed to the right people in the right way. Curiously, this is the point, step 7, when you should go back to Chapter 1 of this book to start plotting how HMRC does not end up being the major beneficiary of your hopefully-it-won't-be-happening-soon demise.

Enjoy Life (the most important step): Life isn't a dress-rehearsal. Paying a bit too much IHT is not catastrophic since you'd pay a lot more than that to spend just one more day on earth with your family and loved ones, so do keep everything in perspective; nobody should pay too much tax - but everybody should enjoy life.

CHAPTER 10

Apocalypse Now
(Common mistakes with Inheritance Tax Planning)

"Experience is simply the name we give our mistakes" — Oscar Wilde, author, poet and playwright.

Not doing anything/Leaving it too late – nobody wants to die and everyone thinks they are going to live forever, so nothing gets started until the last minute when, catastrophically, it is often too late.

No Wills/LPAs – the world of intestacy is a fool's paradise, trying to be fair and pleasing everyone, then failing to achieve both. Not having a will could lead to so many problems that a **Deed of Variation** just cannot correct. Not having LPAs could lead to significant challenges for your loved ones in your final years (*see Chap. 5*).

Gifts with Reservation of Benefits – you cannot have your cake and eat it. If you gift something away, you cannot continue to use it as if it was still your own personal property (*see Chap. 6*).

Incorrect Documentation – unsigned wills, incorrectly set up and unregistered trusts .... with all the best intentions in the world, if they are not executed correctly they become redundant. So make sure you use professionals who know how to complete the forms properly and have suitable insurance in case something goes wrong.

Lack of Documentation – with HMRC you are guilty until you prove otherwise. For every step on the journey, each gift and every transfer, make sure it is documented and that documentation is kept.

Not using exemptions - £3,000 per year over ten years for a couple is a lot of money. It is also a lot of unnecessary Inheritance Tax [£3,000 x 10 years = £30,000 x a couple = £60,000 @ 40% = £24,000) (*see Chap. 6*).

Forgetting inter-spousal transfers – any gifts between spouses and civil partners are exempt from both Capital Gains, as well as Inheritance taxes. So if one is older than the other, then it makes sense for the younger to be making substantial gifts (on the assumption they have the greater life expectancy), meaning the asset is passed from older spouse to younger first. Just make sure it is all properly documented (*see Chap. 4)*.

Allowing unused income to build-up – I see this a lot, especially with the most elderly of individuals who, as they get older spend less and less, while their pension income continues to go up year after year (*see Chap.6*).

No trust with IHT – especially with life assurance policies set up by mortgage brokers, which means on death any payout may go back into the estate to be subject to IHT at 40%.

Too much trust – poorly timed and coordinated PETs and setting up of trusts could mean gifts from as long ago as 14 years being dragged back into the estate to be part of any IHT calculations (*see Chap.6*).

Forgetting the Ten Year Charge – every ten years HMRC levy a tax charge of 6% on the value of the trust assets (to the extent that they are worth more than the available nil band) to make up for the fact they last in perpetuity so IHT could, in theory, could only be levied on them once a century. The most common IHT since even if people know about it, they forget to do it (*see Chap.6*).

Incorrect Charitable-Giving wording in Wills – many people like to gift part of their wealth away to charitable causes on death, especially since it may reduce their IHT rate to 36%. However, incorrectly worded may mean not just qualifying for the reduced rate, but also having your beneficiaries needing to deal with a Charity's solicitors who are demanding that their amount is not reduced as a result of a clerical error (*see Chap.5*).

Getting Equity Release wrong – equity release is a powerful way of releasing cash from a main residence, but since the interest is rolled up it is never totally clear what the net value of everything will be at death. The Residential Nil Rate Band (RNRB) is currently £175,000 for 2025/26, but if the main residence is worth £300,000 and the outstanding equity release mortgage is, for example, £150,000 on death, then the net value of the property is [£300,000 - £150,00 =] £150,000 meaning you cannot use all the available £175,000 (*see Chap. 8*).

Fools' Gold – any scheme that promises overly-complicated, expensive and 'too good to be true' solutions are probably all of these. The lesson of Family Protection Trusts in *Chapter 6* should always be heeded by any shrewd operator in IHT planning.

Not working with a Financial Adviser – the list of errors DIY investors/financial planners make is a long one. I admire anyone who tries to master finances in their spare time – it takes me a full-time job to do it! Therefore, find a

Financial Adviser you like, who you trust (preferably one that is been recommended to you) and ask if they do Cashflow Modelling for every client – if they do, then you are half way there.

CHAPTER 11

The Future

"What's to come is still unsure" – 'Twelfth Night' by William Shakespeare, English playwright

Nobody knows how Inheritance Tax is going to change in the future.

What we do know, however, is that it will.

If you would like to be kept up-to-date with these inevitable, albeit occasional, changes to Inheritance Tax and how it may impact upon you, then head over to my website at lwdfs.co.uk and register for free updates, as and when they happen, or click on this QR code to be taken to the relevant place:

Epilogue: final words

"The greatest use of life is to spend it for something that will outlast it" — William James (1842-1910), US philosopher, widely regarded as the Father of American Psychology.

As mentioned right at the start of this book, this text is not aimed at making the reader an expert in Inheritance Tax planning. Truth be told, because every person's situation is unique and since everything is seemingly changing all the time, be that due to meddling ministers in government or changing interpretations of the rules by HMRC, it is genuinely hard for anyone to claim such a label. However, while nothing can replace the carefully accumulated knowledge of an experienced practitioner of the craft and their years of hard-graft, after reading this miniature tome I hope you, the reader, now has a little more knowledge and perhaps a bit more confidence to start your own journey towards getting your affairs arranged in such a way to protecting your own wealth. After all, nobody wants to leave a huge bulk of their estate to HMRC when they die.

In my experience, most clients like to include their beneficiaries when making these plans so that they can find out how any legacy can help them the most, such as repaying debts, funding education, or even helping them to retire. It is never easy to start a conversation with your loved ones about what may happen when you pass away, especially one which also involves money, but once they have started it can be surprisingly rewarding, with the peace of mind that everyone has clarity about what happens next. Even better, if you're doing this with the expert guidance of a Financial Adviser, they would be there as well when it happens to support your loved ones, helping with the admin and guiding them too. I often say to my clients that, in many respects, the work I will do for them in the twelve months after they have departed this mortal coil, will often be more valuable than the work I had done in the twelve years preceding it. In the end, everyone just needs to be like Lord Dave:

Going to see my client Lord Dave in Hammersmith is always a joy. It always struck me as strange as I left the tube station to the hustle and bustle at the heart of a capital city for the brief walk to his house, when turning down a road off a busy high street would then lead to another, leafy and quiet, as if you had suddenly stepped into suburbia. Lord Dave's house is situated on a corner to one of these side roads and has on its premises something very rare – unique, even - in London, that money cannot buy and people would happily kill for: a garage - which is somewhat ironic, since Lord Dave doesn't own a car. Of course, he isn't a real Lord and I had no idea why he is so named, nor even why his email contained such a title, but sometimes these questions need to remain unanswered. Lord Dave is not a native to these sceptred isles, but his command of the English language is extraordinary, as perhaps befitting a retired English teacher who fills his days of retirement by privately tutoring youngsters who aspired to excel in English at school. Living alone in this huge house with its empty garage, I always wondered why there were so many umbrellas by the coat stand in the dark, mahogany-panelled hallway of his home, so I fondly imagined that maybe they belonged to various Mary Poppinses who had left them there after popping in for a cup of tea with a spoon full of sugar. Usually, as I made my way to his study past walls displaying rare prints and shelves of even rarer first editions of classic literature, the ensuing conversations were nearly always the same, about which Shakespeare text was being taught at GCSE that year, how his various investments had performed, as well as a tentative discussions on IHT planning which never seemed to go anywhere. Eventually, though, the message got through when I received the following email, written in typical Lord Dave fashion:

"I wept when I read your report, not least since you consistently fail to observe the subjunctive in counterfactual conditionals — and don't get me started on your unthinking genitive apostrophes in non-possessive plural constructions! However, I do get that you are telling me that I may have a potential Inheritance Tax problem – perhaps we could start putting some plans in place next time we meet?"

The moral of this book, then ? Be like Lord Dave!

About the author

'Try not to become a man of success, but rather try to become a man of value' – Albert Einstein

Lee Denham is an experienced Financial Adviser and Chartered Associate of the London Institute of Banking and Finance, who has worked in the financial services industry since 1998 at both advisory and management level. Based in Watford for most of his life, he attended the local Grammar School for Boys before embarking on a career in retail and then finance, in particular specialising in Pension and Retirement planning, as well as Inheritance Tax mitigation.

When taking on clients, his aim is to work closely with each of them to produce a financial plan that takes into account both their values and goals, thus helping them discover the meaning of *true wealth* – which is something that money cannot buy and what death cannot take away. What money cannot buy is peace of mind, which is a personalised financial plan that is structured in such a way that guides people towards the life they want to lead, and what Death cannot take away, is a plan that ensures their wishes are honoured long after they're gone. We call it Legacy Financial Planning™ and believe nobody else delivers financial advice quite like this, that makes sure you never run out of money during your lifetime, as well as ensuring you leave the legacy you truly want at the end.

Away from the office, he is the proud husband of Anna and their two boys. He is also an advocate of opera and symphonic music, in particular contributing articles and reviews to the online classical music site, *MusicWeb*

International, as well as being a keen cook. As a result of the latter, he does his best to keep his ever-expanding waistline in check by occasionally mustering enough energy to enter races, triathlons and marathons, helping to raise funds for charity.

Lee Denham can be contacted at: lwdfs.co.uk

Acknowledgements

'*Gratitude is the sign of noble souls*' – Aesop

First and foremost, many thanks and much adoration must go to my endlessly patient wife, Anna, who must wonder what it is like to have a husband who is not always tapping away on his laptop. Sadly, she may never find out …

As well to Pat Williams, Richard Cowling, Gary Bunce, Keith Humphrey and Joe Papworth who all helped begin my career in finance many years back and whose support is still gratefully remembered. As is that of Gabriel Rooney who, like me, forgot his tie for our first meeting – we were clearly destined to work together. In particular, special mention must also be given to Pastor Mark Hobbs of the New Leaf Distribution network – never has the tale of the footsteps in the sand been more relevant.

I would like to thank my friend and editor at *MusicWeb International*, Ralph Moore, who kindly agreed to check and edit this text. His fee, usually measured in alcohol, is ridiculously cheap, but I fear even the load of champagne I sent him on this occasion will never be enough for him to fully recover from this latest ordeal at my hands. Any mistakes which remain in the text though, are mine and mine alone.

Likewise, David Young, a native of St Helena and valued client, who agreed to be one of my beta-readers and in doing so re-organised the text with an appropriately Napoleonesque battle-plan cunning, as well as Kim Luckhurst who made sure that (so far) my written word has not fallen foul of merciless eye of the regulator.

But most of all I would like to thank my clients, without whom this book would have been possible. Generously, they have all contributed to the text and patiently, they have always entertained me as I strived to do my best with their finances and plan for their futures. It is a privilege to work with them all.

In memory to all my clients who, sadly, have come to the end of their Inheritance Tax planning journeys: Jim, Dimitri, Tip, Frances, Kath, Jeff, Brian, Rose, John and David - gone but not forgotten.

Notes

1) Will writing and advice on Lasting Powers of Attorney are not regulated by the Financial Conduct Authority

2) Trusts are not regulated by the Financial Conduct Authority

3) The value of investments and any income from them can fall as well as rise, and you may get back less than you invest. Past performance is not a reliable indicator of future results.

4) All insurance policies are subject to eligibility, exclusions, and terms and conditions. If you stop paying your premiums, your cover will end, and your policy may have no cash-in value.

5) Equity release and other lifetime mortgage, as well as Retirement Interest-Only Mortgages are loans secured against your home. It will reduce the value of your estate and may affect your entitlement to means-tested benefits.Your home may be repossessed if you do not keep up repayments on your mortgage or any other debt secured on it.

Glossary of terms

1. **Absolute Trust:** (also known as a bare trust) is a simple trust where the beneficiaries and their shares are fixed from the start — the trustees look after the assets, but have no discretion over who gets what or when.
2. **Agricultural Relief:** A relief reducing the taxable value of agricultural property for IHT purposes.
3. **AIM shares:** Shares of smaller companies that are entitled to Business Property Relief.
4. **Annual Exemption:** The amount individuals can give away each tax year without it being included in their estate for IHT purposes (currently £3,000 per year).
5. **Bare Trust:** A trust where the beneficiary is absolutely entitled to the trust assets.
6. **Beneficiary:** A person who benefits from the estate or trust.
7. **Business Relief (BR):** A relief reducing the taxable value of certain business assets, potentially down to 0%, for IHT purposes (formerly referred to as Business Property Relief – BPR)
8. **Chargeable Estate:** The portion of an estate that exceeds the combined NRB and RNRB allowances, subject to IHT.
9. **Charitable Gifts Exemption:** Gifts left to UK charities, which are exempt from IHT. Estates leaving at least 10% to charity may benefit from a reduced IHT rate of 36%.
10. **Death Certificate:** A legal document that proves the passing of the deceased, required by banks, insurance companies, etc to release funds and cooperate with those administering the estate.
11. **Deed of Variation:** A legal document that allows beneficiaries to alter a will after the testator's death to

achieve more favourable tax treatment or redistribute the estate.

12. **Deemed Domicile:** A tax status where an individual is treated as domiciled in the UK for IHT purposes, even if they are not formally domiciled, typically after living in the UK for 15 of the last 20 years.

13. **Discounted Gift Plan:** a financial arrangement designed to reduce potential Inheritance Tax while allowing the donor to retain a guaranteed income for life.

14. **Discretionary Trust:** A trust where trustees have the authority to decide how the trust income and capital are distributed.

15. **Domicile:** The country where a person has their permanent home, impacting IHT liability.

16. **Equity Release:** Allows homeowners (usually over 55) to borrow money against the value of their home. The loan and any interest is typically repaid from the estate after death, reducing the inheritance.

17. **Estate**: The total value of all assets and property owned by a person at the time of their death, minus any liabilities.

18. **Excluded Property:** Assets that are not subject to IHT, such as foreign assets owned by a non-UK domicile.

19. **Executors:** Individuals named in a will who are responsible for administering the estate.

20. **Exempt Beneficiary:** Individuals or entities to whom assets can be left without incurring IHT, such as a spouse or civil partner.

21. **Family Investment Companies (FICO):** a private company set up to hold and manage family wealth, allowing parents to transfer value to children through share structures while retaining control, so that future growth falls outside their estate for UK Inheritance Tax purposes.

22. **Family Investment LLP:** as above, except within the structure of a limited liability partnership.

23. **Gift and Loan Plan:** an IHT strategy where you give a lump sum to a trust for your beneficiaries and also lend a separate sum to the trust interest-free, which is then repaid over a period of time, providing a tax free income.

24. **Gift inter Vivos:** A form of insurance that covers any potential liability that a donee may be liable for when receiving a large gift from someone's estate and the donor then dies within seven years (i.e. therefore a failed Potentially Exempt Transfer (PET).

25. **Gifts with Reservation:** Is the term used to describe the ownership of an asset being passed from person to another, where the first person continues to enjoy the beneficial ownership of the asset. In these circumstances, HMRC will continue to assume the asset remains part of the donor's estate for IHT purposes.

26. **Grant of Probate:** The legal document authorizing executors to deal with the deceased's estate.

27. **Gross Estate:** The total value of all assets before deducting liabilities and IHT allowances.

28. **IHT205:** Form that is sent to HMRC for small, non-taxable estates to obtain Grant of Probate.

29. **IHT400:** Form that is sent to HMRC for taxable, or complex estates to obtain Grant of Probate.

30. **Inheritance Tax (IHT):** A tax on the estate of someone who has died, including all property, possessions, and money.

31. **Intestate:** Dying without a valid will, resulting in the estate being distributed according to statutory rules.

32. **Joint Tenants:** (as opposed to Tenants In Common) is a form of property ownership whereby each owner owns the whole property jointly (rather than a specific share) and if one owner dies, their share automatically passes to the other(s).

33. **Letters of Wishes:** accompanies a trust giving guidance to the trustees as to how the trust's assets should be distributed.

34. **Lifetime Gift:** A gift given during a person's lifetime, which may be subject to IHT if the giver dies within seven years of the gift.

35. **Net Estate:** The value of an estate after deducting liabilities and IHT allowances.

36. **Nil-Rate Band (NRB):** The threshold up to which an estate is not subject to IHT. As of 2024, this is set at £325,000.

37. **Potentially Exempt Transfer (PET):** A gift made during a person's lifetime that may become exempt from IHT if the giver survives for seven years after making the gift.

38. **Probate:** The legal process of administering a deceased person's estate.

39. **Residence Nil-Rate Band (RNRB):** An additional IHT allowance for a person's main residence if passed to direct descendants, such as children or grandchildren.

40. **Settlor:** The person who creates a trust by placing assets into it.

41. **Small Gifts Exemption:** Gifts of up to £250 per person per tax year that are exempt from IHT.

42. **Spousal Exemption:** Unlimited IHT exemption for transfers of assets between spouses or civil partners.

43. **Taper Relief:** A reduction in IHT on gifts made between three and seven years before death.

44. **Tenants in Common:** (as opposed to Joint Tenants) is a form of property ownership whereby each owner holds a distinct share property (e.g. 50/50 or 70/30) and there is no right of survivorship — each person's share passes under their Will or intestacy.

45. **Testator:** the general term given to a person setting-up a trust.

46. **Trustee:** A person or entity responsible for managing a trust in accordance with the trust deed.

www.ingramcontent.com/pod-product-compliance
Lightning Source LLC
LaVergne TN
LVHW022308200926
848481LV00004B/1243
9781918424577